ISBN: 978-1-0881-1316-5

Stephen R. Andrew
25 Middle Street
Portland, Maine 04101
www.hetimaine.org

Author's note

To be present with people is to listen deeply and try to get a "felt sense" of what it is like to be them. You know you're doing it well when you, at least briefly, lose the sense of yourself and are consumed only with an understanding of the person you're trying to serve. You merge into the spirit of another human being, then differentiate, then do that over and over.

Stephen R. Cohen

Acknowledgements

I would love to thank dearly people who shaped me both personally and professionally~ Melissa, Doug, Kelley, Doreen, Alice, Mary C., Dan C., Oliver B., John B., Bob J., Linda J., David P., Marie S., Angelina M., Brian C., Elizabeth M. L. , Sarah F., Gabrielle R. T., Michael N., Max H., Michael M., Neil M., Rodney, Jill F., Bill M., Terri M., Susan D., Alan L., David P., Gracelynn., Stefan, Billy V., Geoff K., Dottie F., Alexandra H., Donna D., Kym D., Lacey S., Susan C., Tom C. Stan E., Mindy, Dino, Brad K., Li B., friends in the MINT community and all the people in our support groups in the last 35 years...all of the donors to and board members of our nonprofit, Agape Inc., InnerEdge and Dignity ...

Hilary, Sebastian, Jeff S. Deborah S., Coral S., Joan A., John P. Susan P, Michael P., Blaine H., Alison C., Christine M., Gilda N., Anita K., and the Kindred Spirits & Heartquest community.

Listening Deeply

Let me start with this idea — **we change people through the heart, not the mind**. That is, helping people requires first listening for what they most *yearn*. As a helper and a provider of helping support services, we try to start my conversations, including this one with you, with a simple phrase, more of a prayer, sometimes spoken, often not, but always central before I begin: "I am here for you" or "May I be of service to acceptance and compassion."

Next comes the moment of **listening deeply**. As someone addresses you, your eyes and ears see and hear what they are saying, and those senses send the seeing and hearing to your mind, where it crystallizes. Often at this precise point, things go wrong, and you feel a desire to solve the difficulty being expressed or move away from the suffering of this person so as to not feel your own mirrored suffering. Once you do that, you are no longer really in partnership with the person you are serving or being with.

How do you take what people say when you ask an open-ended question – "How are you doing?" or "Tell me what's going on with your diabetes?" – and then listen with the *heart*? In taking in the answer, it's normal to reflect on your own life experiences. Again, put those thoughts gently aside. Imagine your *lived experience* and *solutions* passing through your mind and then dropping into your heart and then you respond, *what must they be thinking, what must they be feeling?* This is how people who are suffering feel heard and believed. An empathetic statement,

This kind of dialogue gets especially difficult when you hear things you disagree with. A judgment within you is attached when you listen with your mind to correct or defend. Instead, move gently to your heart, where your internal reviewer falls away and what remains is a felt sense and yearning behind the words.

This empathetic way of listening has completely changed my work. The (My) goal for this kind of helping in support settings is to have a "felt sense" of what it must be like to be the people we serve, to hear and believe their experiences through authentic empathetic understanding, which I've come to see as the most helpful process to another human being.

Practicing empathetic understanding is a dance that goes something like this:

1. Receive the response from another person, both non-verbally and verbally.

2. Bring it to your heart and consider what it's like to be them or *what they must be thinking, what must they be feeling?* Seeking a "felt sense" below the words. Listen for the whisper of the other one's values, hopes, and dreams.

3. Respond with a *gentle guess* that starts by naming that felt sense.

4. Watch how your response lands, specifically how it travels through their own life experiences, their historical residue, likely very different from yours. Stay attuned to the reactions.

5. Repeat the process going ever so closer to accurate authentic empathy, a knowing each other in this moment.

The 'pesky' ego and compassion fatigue

If you're exhausted from helping people, perhaps instead of offering thoughts and feelings of empathetic understanding and developing a partnership, you are taking what people say to you and then feeling responsible for fixing, solving a problem, or delivering an outcome. This may be the role you had in your family of origin, the caretaker. Or you are putting your need to be understood first, to feel good internally before truly empathetically understanding the person before you. This is power over and it restimulates the original "hurts" of the other person. We would call that our "pesky ego", which we all possess and is more interested in holding a correct, "right" position than in understanding others. A valuable thought is: **Holding a "right" position is to destroy the relationship**. Much of our anxiety and inner turmoil comes from living in a culture of values that drives us away from our heart. This creates a "pesky ego". At the heart of this is the conflict between an outer definition of success and an inner value of peace and compassion.

Unfortunately, we are encouraged, even trained, to get attention and affirmations, when the real secret of life is to give loving and undivided dignity to others.

In the process of performing well on a test, positioning ourselves for a promotion, or competing on athletic fields, we are schooled to believe that to succeed we must get attention, validation, and be recognized as more than another. When, actually, the importance of all that is extraordinary in life opens only when we devote ourselves to giving loving attention, not getting it.

Things come alive for us only when we dare to give unconditional empathy and compassion. The longer we have tried to get attention rather than giving it, the deeper our unhappiness and suffering. This leads us to move through the world dreaming, hoping for greatness, needing to be validated at every turn.

Feelings of oneness grace us only when we are validated by the life around us. It makes us desperate to feel loved, when we sorely need the medicine of being loving.

One reason that so many of us are lonely and isolated in this dream of success rather than looking for what is clear and true is that we learn to covet power. Another reason we live so far from peace and compassion is that instead of loving our way into joy, we think that affirmation and fame will soothe us.

While we are busy dreaming of being famous, being a celebrity, being more important than others we stifle our need to see beauty and to give love. This leaves us with the choices: be a celebrity or celebrate being, be seen or devoting ourselves to seeing the other, fame or peace in our heart, building our identity on the affirmations and attention we get or finding the beauty of things and people through giving loving attention. Our ambivalence, our choice

For example, with a person who has diabetes, you may want to tell, suggest, advise that they are eating poorly. You likely want to tell them what your brain knows, and is probably true, that their behavior is unhealthy. This is a simply our "pesky ego" interrupting our goal of empathetic understanding. Now you are in internal conflict because your heart wants to connect, and your mind wants to solve the person's suffering.

Consider every individual you meet as *a garden to be tended, not a machine to be repaired*. Approach conversations as a mechanic thinking, "I must fix this," and prepare to get psychically greasy, covered in a mess of increasing anxiety and disconnection between yourself and the other. When you enter a conversation instead as a gardener, seeking only to cultivate the plot of land (their narrative), the seeds of connection have a better chance, a higher probability, of growing. Our eventual harvest will be people we serve who accept themselves and dream aloud to help themselves. It is the connection that insulates from the toxic shame and promotes the belief within of their own resiliency.

Your heart lives in the now and is generally bereft of judgment about the future. Instead, it is responsible for life-giving action at this moment in time. As a provider or as just a listener to a friend, leading from the heart avoids fatigue about how the person will live their life in all of those tomorrows. Heart-centric listening is the best medicine, delivering benefits to both sides the helper and person we serve. Listening deeply to the whisper of the human soul is not a burden, it's a wonderful opportunity.

Just being present is increasingly tricky given the demands on helpers these days, including perceived defined outcomes. Still, a part of you likely knows that what people need, at least initially, is connection, *empathetic understanding*. No matter our subsequent trauma, stigmatization, or oppression, we all initially arrive on this planet to love well and to connect deeply. That's why we're here in this moment. The absence of connection makes nearly all chronic illnesses worse and so has actual large-scale negative epidemiological outcomes, including reduced life expectancy. Now is the time to embrace empathetic understanding, always the precursor to changing lives and increasing resiliency. It will inspire the people we serve.

Empathy and countertransference

We are (I am) sometimes asked about the relationship between empathy and countertransference, which is the transferring of a helper's thoughts and feelings onto the person we serve. Since practicing compassion, **the ability to sit with another suffering**, requires forgetting one's own spirit even exists, this softens the effects of countertransference, which is the "pesky ego". "I need to solve this, to come up with a solution, a suggestion and be even more curious." Unsure of what to say, we go to self-disclosure, our story, often referred to as "sympathy".

These power-over thoughts get in the way of helping others, so the more of them you have, the greater the urgency to move toward empathetic understanding, which like a muscle needs to get exercised regularly and repeatedly. When empathetic understanding is not being used, chances are you, as the helper, are lost in your own material and life experiences instead of being with them, the person we serve.

To avoid getting lost, before seeing them, I (We can) take a deep breath and focus inwards on an internal prayer; "I am here for you" which sometimes my own internal dialogue says, "May I be of service to acceptance and compassion." These internal chants keep me focused on the *work* I am supposed to be doing, which is to honor the person in front of me and their perception of the world; and along the way, helping them to address a chronic illness or suffering.

Listening Deeply is a full-body experience. You use your eyes, ears, mind, and heart, the latter being the source of empathy. How well do we practice this? It's a big question, as helping needs to be more accountable regarding success in providing genuine compassion, authentic empathy. We know that 30% of helpers in the field are doing harm by giving toxic shame thinking, believing that is empathetic understanding, which leads to resistance, hostility, and an increase in hopelessness among people, who, in the end, do not move forward in their lives and their own hopes and dreams of connection. *STUCK!*.

We must be accountable for empathy & compassion, especially in a world with arguably too much accountability for outcomes. It is bizarre that one can get through social work, nursing, or medical school often without demonstrating a single empathetic conversation. Returning to our gardening metaphor, all of these helper professions are trying to grow a garden by just throwing the seeds on top of the soil without cultivating the ground underneath. Health won't grow very well in these conditions. So, the fundamental first step in any interaction with a person you serve is developing empathetic understanding with a gentle cadence of open-ended questions and deep listening.

What about the people we serve who want us to "fix it"? Do you believe wholeheartedly that *if people naturally come up with their own ideas, they are more likely to follow through*? I observe that if I offer a solution, the response often is "yes, but...," which means that they do not think that they can do it; that although they are looking for power and control over the destiny of their lives, they don't believe in themselves. If you hear those words, you have gone too fast, too far in pushing the person to change, and they're not ready. So back up and cultivate the ground.

We shift how we respond when asked for specific advice. "I can answer that" to, "I'd like to answer that and the truth is, if you come up with your own ideas and solutions for solving this struggle within, you're more likely to follow through because that solution fits your values and who you are." While we might talk about what we would do, this will not necessarily help the person posing the question. Instead, we respond with a more open-ended question, "We wonder what you are thinking about?" — and then it's back to the practice of empathetic understanding with the guiding focus on creating an energetic space where you connect in peace. This is known as accurate empathy; connection promotes core needs to be fulfilled.

Unlearning old patterns

As a helper, you may face challenges in silencing your "pesky ego" and its desire to take over and tell people what to do. That ego likely comes from your whole life experience that has gently molded you into a role of caretaker. Perhaps growing up, you were the one the family relied on for help, and you learned and practiced and became one and were happy to do so. Caretaking gave you a purpose. Caretakers often marry someone they can care for and have children who demand still more caretaking. Then often they will find a job where they can earn money caring for others. So, your orientation as a *fixer* is an old pattern, and old habits can be difficult to change.

Your "pesky ego" might say, "Based on your diabetes, Mr. Dodge, you need to lower your sugar levels," to which Mr. Dodge may respond, "Well, I think I am doing enough." Now you're struggling, as your ego wants to fight for the correct position, persuade or sell health, and begin designing a plan – "I want you to be healthy here, so if you would do a little more this week." But Mr. Dodge is resistant and will not do more this week since it wasn't his plan in the first place. If the situation demands advice, an alternative approach is asking permission via an open-ended question, reinforcing the idea that Mr. Dodge has power and control, autonomy over his life. "What do you think about this?" Practice a cycle of asking permission and leaning into giving our power away to them, "May I give you some ideas about things you may do that other people in your situation have tried?"

Another challenge to focusing on the gift of presence comes from the broader culture which is highly competitive and laser-focused on intellect and education and often undervalues those who work closest to the heart, who work with empathetic understanding. There's a belief that people need us to hold them accountable. One way we have endeavored to change this is by developing learning communities to practice connection. These are weekly one-hour group meetings to practice empathetic understanding, and to eschew unsolicited advice and problem-solving altogether. ***Unsolicited advice, problem-solving, unasked-for suggestions are a form of violence, emotional violence.*** **"I know that you do not know."**

Here's how a practice of empathy might work with Mr. Dodge: "I can see how important it is for you to have that mince pie because it is part of your legacy, your mother baked for you out of love, and you want that delicious pie and love, no matter the consequences."

We've empathized with their need for the pie and allowed for an opening for them to say, "I know the consequences are not very good." We've moved them delicately towards thinking aloud about another way into their healing process.

The top five lessons that we have learned in our empathy and compassion work and practice are:

1. It's possible to still challenge a person to grow using feedback and mirroring that is grounded in empathy and compassion.

2. One of my favorite lines from my first book *Love in Action, Art of Compassionate Helping* is: **I believe that we should meet people where they dream, and not from the perspective that there is something wrong with them that needs fixing. We should stop meeting them where they're at,**

but meet them where they long to be.

3. When a helper, therapist, social worker, or really anyone who has "power over" another dismisses or controls them, it stifles their growth, is shaming, and can cause harm.

4. People usually know inside what they need, want, and hope for. Unsolicited advice can serve to cover this over, is often unwanted, and misses the real opportunity to simply see, hear, and accept them just as they are, which is the ground of real healing.

5. Resistance in the helper relationship is not usually coming from the person we serve, but from the helpers not accepting and

having an empathetic understanding of where the person is. When we stop trying to force change on people, we finally see them clearly, their trust in us grows, and healing is possible. Our "pesky ego" needs to be kept in check.

To be present with people is to **listen deeply** and try to get a "felt sense" of what it is like to be them. You know you're doing it well when you at least briefly lose the sense of yourself and are consumed only with an understanding of the person you're trying to serve. You merge into the spirit of another human being, then differentiate, then do that over and over. This is the rhythm of the connection in an encounter. Just like the breath – you go in, touch with empathy, merge and then you go out and shift back to yourself again. We promise that connecting this way is energizing and will not tire you. Your fatigue today likely stems from trying to fix people. Deep presence and compassion are associated with the sought-after flow state and zest for any work, including helping another human being even with the most difficult stories.

Helpers commonly stumble over three obstacles to this sort of deep presence:

1. **Giving unsolicited advice**. The problem here is not the advice, but the unsolicited nature, which is reactive rather than proactive. To

be proactive is to hear a person's suffering, sit with it, and hold it with care. Only then ask if they would be open to some ideas. This precursor increases the chance that these ideas will land on the person in a way that makes them feel valued and important, that they are the most important focus in the room, certainly above any service plan or entries on endless required forms that accompany treatment.

2. **Posing a series of questions.** Three questions or more in a row is a trap. By asking them, you're pulling the harvest towards you before it's ready. If you harvest a garden before it's ready, it dies. The rule is our of practice empathy should

outpace asking questions by at least a 2:1 ratio. A question is a demand while empathy is a gift. Empathy is putting money in an emotional trust fund between you and another person. We have many questions, especially given contemporary practice of helping. Still, we are asking helpers in social services to spend the first ten to fifteen minutes when meeting someone intentionally practicing empathetic understanding and resisting asking any questions except open-ended, inviting questions. Look them in the eye and say, "How can I support you?" or perhaps, "I have this information from your doctor, and I'd love to know what you think about it ." After a period of empathetic understanding, you can move into more specific, pragmatic questions, but even then, only with permission. Interestingly, we now know that patients are twice as honest with us in those intake forms after we've done the ten minutes of cultivating the ground.

3. **Making excessive self-disclosures.** This is when we make it about us rather than them, a classic sympathy-not-empathy mistake that can be excessively hurtful. Here's a quick story about a person we have served that illustrates the point. This person's wife passed away when she was just 42. He is a physician and took a month off after her passing to grieve. I saw

him after he returned to work and he talked of hearing two basic things from his colleagues and co-workers: "I'm so sorry for your loss...life will get better" and, "I know what you're going through, I've just lost my brother." This person had no capacity to listen to somebody else, either opinion or self-disclosure. He needed someone to look him in the eye and say, "You're going through a lot, perhaps you'd like some support," which is empathy. Self-disclosure comes from that "pesky ego" again and our uncertainty about how to engage empathetically. Sympathy is "I'm sorry," while empathy is, "You're sad about the loss of your wife." Attempts, even at gentle empathy, can go wrong if a person disagrees and says he feels another way. That clarification gives me more of his story, so the risk was worth it. It takes vulnerability to reflect a felt sense, so your vulnerability can be a doorway to the real story and is vital in listening deeply.

One way to inoculate yourself against these obstacles is simply repeating, *I am responsible for the intervention, not the outcome*. More specifically, focusing on the intervention is about returning to three practices. First, engage with a high level of empathy. Second, fully hear the dilemma and struggle, and then use empathetic reflections about that struggle and the felt sense behind it.

Third, wonder aloud with them about what they want to do with that struggle. These practices cultivate the ground and help the person you are serving plant seeds that they will eventually harvest; their hopes and dreams.

Similarly, in a garden it's your plants that ultimately deliver the harvest, though it will be more fruitful the more you tend the environment in which they grow through regular watering, weeding, fertilizing, and thinning. The key here is that the most proximate cause of any eventual lasting outcome is the person coming up with and acting on their own ideas. Even if they don't have ideas, when you get to that last third of the conversation, you can make a gentle invitation to the notion of harvest, as we mentioned earlier, by just saying, "Would you be open to an idea that I think might be helpful based on what we've heard?" Offer the idea and then ask them what they think about it. A gentle cycle of *ask-offer-ask* can move them toward change if the time is right. You'll know you're too soon if you sense seeds flying around and not taking hold. You'll likely realize you're wasting your time and theirs, and you'll undoubtedly be even more exhausted.

Risk-taking adolescents

Earlier in my career, I ran a group home for seven years for chemically dependent adolescents. It was then that I first learned the importance of connection and relationships. I recall research at the time in which the U.S. government asked young people, five years after they had left group homes, what they most remembered that the group homes had taught them. Of course, they could not recall anything except the names of the people who had influenced them the most.

Being a positive influence in a group home setting requires two key ingredients – empathy and boundaries. Ideally, you lead with compassion, though in a facility where you are responsible for protocol, setting boundaries follows closely behind. Safety issues may require you to reverse the order, boundary first, then empathy. If it's not unsafe, always start with the heart. This guidance is tough to follow. Too often, helpers gets caught in their countertransference about losing power and control, so they always get into boundaries and limit-setting, which precludes establishing relationships that influence the self-determination of young people.

This lesson applies far beyond institutional settings to most relationships, including your role as a parent or caregiver. First, cultivate empathy, and then set compassionate boundaries. It doesn't matter what relationship it is – a parent or a caregiver. When there is conflict, jumping straight to, "Here's what I expect" is unlikely to yield lasting change. In a tense group home environment, it takes real effort to pause and begin with empathetic understanding. Helpers get hooked by the person's often outrageous actions and react by selling health, admonishing behavior change, giving unsolicited advice, or using other strategies to get the person to do something different and follow the rules or even common sense – none of which ever works. What does work is the slow process of building trust, emotional intimacy, and empathy.

I love the phrase **Empathy is the only antidote to shame**. That is, you cannot ask questions or give information that will reduce a person's shame. The only way is through empathetic understanding, which means making those gentle guesses about the felt sense behind what the person is saying to you. Don't repeat what they say, but probe with phrases like "If I were you, I'd be feeling" or "If I were you, I'd be thinking."

Interventions

Many of us work with people facing dire circumstances that demand immediate change, such as severe alcohol and other drug misuse or recurring and specific thoughts of suicide. Even and perhaps especially in such cases, your task is a slow and intentional one of working through several steps – engage thoughtfully, find the conflict between where they are and what they wish for, and perhaps most important, address the profound toxic shame that is so often present.

Shame has three components, some combination of which you'll observe in many interactions with the people we serve, particularly those who have been hurt. The first is isolation. The feeling is, "I don't trust the world so I will keep to myself." This is often experienced by older people experiencing ageism and being left alone. The second shame component is a value conflict, evident in the "I want this, and do that" pattern. This is common in people with a substance use disorder who might say, "I want to be clean and sober, and I don't or can't stop drinking and using." The third component, which I think is the most important and damaging, is the loss of empathy for self and others. Therefore, the engagement phase is so essential, in which you focus on offering empathetic understanding and communicating "you matter" through empathetic understanding and acceptance. It is our primary intention to hear their hopes and dreams, this often drowns out the trauma whispers of the person we are serving.

Trauma comes from many different places – whether from experiences growing up or the communities in which a person has lived. For example, someone with a learning disability or who otherwise has some characteristic that makes it difficult to fit in might experience trauma. Indeed, since most of us have experienced a sense of not belonging, perhaps we all carry some version of the trauma whisper. It's lodged deep, really incorporated into our tissues and cells. Hence, as you approach somebody, their entire body begins to get anxious and the mind starts whispering phrases like, "I don't matter," "I am not lovable," and "The world is not to be trusted."

When you are sitting with somebody, their whisper will also be audible to you. For example, they may say, "It doesn't matter if I do it or not" (I don't matter), or, "Nobody cares about what happens to me" (I'm not loveable), or, "You folks are always trying to push something on me" (The world is not to be trusted).

Trauma is made up of both specific experiences and generalized oppression based on culture, race, sexual orientation, intellectual level, economic status, or age; all of which can cause people to feel as though they are not worthy. Though the situation is changing, historically, we didn't discuss oppression within helping professions, we were generally more concerned with acute conditions. One definition of oppression is people with power systematically defining and training the culture what to believe about people with less power. A poor person in a capitalist culture might feel like they don't matter – and thus, this may be part of the trauma you're listening for as a helper. Trauma whispers also come from stigmatization, which makes people feel moral discord about their behavior.

The trauma whisper protects the person from any further toxic shame and they put up an invisible wall. The best way of softening the wall is with empathy, which in turn quiets the toxic shame. After that, you can begin exploring their struggle between what they are doing and what they want to do. Every human being faces the dilemma of listening to their trauma or listening to their hopes and dreams. If you listen well, you'll be able to hear both whispers. Don't judge them. There are no resistant people, only our universal struggle between our heart and our head. If you are experiencing resistance, it's your "pesky ego" wanting them to do something they are not doing. Carry this phrase as an antidote. ***People are doing***

***the best that they can with the resources
they have, and I might be a resource.***

We must listen at an authentic
empathetic level to activate the human
soul's self-determination, resiliency, and
inherent healing capacity. As we have
said earlier, connection is healing for
people, it promotes the quality and
quantity of their life. The greatest
chronic illness is continued *loneliness*.
Connection, social capital, makes
another person calm down anxiety, quiet
their soul, and causes cognitive
dissonance in their brain, their thinking,
which begins to say, "Oh, I matter."
Meeting someone at the soul level, being
present, believing in them, and offering
radical acceptance; people want and

need these connections. They want acceptance for who they are now, an acknowledgment that they are doing their best, and compassion from other people that where they are is okay. *I am doing the absolute best I can at this given moment with the resources I have.*

Another way of saying this is to move gently towards the suffering without giving unsolicited advice or information, asking a series of questions or, giving excessive self-disclosure. This practice of leaning into the hopelessness or despair allows us to stay with the emotional distress and cultivate bravery and courage towards the hopes and dreams of the person.

As a helper, this sort of compassion might be challenging if somebody says to you, as once happened to me, "All I want to do is go to Walmart, get myself a gun, and shoot myself." This scared me, activated my fear, countertransference, and caused me to make a mistake that I'll never forget. I said, "Isn't there any part of you that would like to live?" That is a complete therapeutic and relationship failure. One, I am asking a question and two, I am not listening to the depth of their despair. They wanted me to look at them and say, "You are feeling hopeless right now." I didn't want to do this because I, rather my "pesky ego," was afraid of enabling them getting closer to suicide. The answer to my question from them was "No," so asking it likely did what I most feared. In other words, my "pesky ego" made them feel even more hopeless and think, "Now, here's another person who doesn't want to hear my despair." You'll be doing good work if you can hold people's despair without believing you must fix it.

Healing our fractured discourse

We are in the United States, where public discourse of all kinds is increasingly fractured, as is true in many other countries. Eventually, we could no longer sit back and watch this strife, so we got a grant to develop and publish a podcast, **Conversations in Compassion**, which is now available on most podcast platforms. It is our effort to address the root cause of so many social ills by demonstrating how to have a compassionate conversation with people who have suffered deeply in their lives.

Repairing the fracture in our culture will not be about having the "right position" but rather about empathizing and creating states of compassion with others, no matter how radical their positions. If you can at least initially suspend your opinion and embrace the enemy with empathetic understanding, radical acceptance, and compassion, you are working for the greater good, for connection. We'd go so far as to urge you to consider it as an opportunity to lean towards those people who differ from you as it's a chance to demonstrate what empathetic understanding can do and to experience first-hand what much of the evidence already suggests – that trying to change people's opinions makes them dig their heels in further, while meeting people with empathetic understanding, expands their openness. This is our way out of the hostility, the social ills of our time.

What to do with your anxiety? Talking about politics and culture is hard enough, but it's often scarier to be a helper worrying about their behavior. The advice is simple – when hooked by something in a conversation, the first thing to do is to pause (drop into momentary silence) and breathe deeply, which helps us settle and keeps us from jumping or reacting. The other person also feels respected when we break for a moment. Then it's just going back to the practice cadence with a gentle guess – "If I were you, I'd be feeling" – and an offer of a felt sense. If I can't make such an offer, I am likely in my head, stuck in the dangerous neighborhood of the "pesky ego".

Egos have extraordinary adaptive value, including holding onto vast amounts of practical knowledge, but they must not drive the bus when connection, empathetic understanding, and mindful movement towards accurate empathetic connection is necessary. Think of ego as an acronym – *Easing Goodness Out*. That is, it is pushing away the goodness that could have emerged between two people looking at something together. If *we believe wholeheartedly in them* and we can come to see the problem they are struggling with through their narrative, then we can create a space for collaboration.

Everywhere people have the same yearning for connection, which quiets their anxiety and allows them to look out into the world with different eyes and a different, opening heart.

Everywhere too, there is compassion fatigue which comes from not genuinely operating in empathetic understanding and compassion. **We change people with the heart, not with the mind**. If you are tired from the work, you're driving from your head and mind and seeing things as a mechanic. If we get good at empathy, then magic happens. You feel alive and at your best when your heart takes over from your mind, and it is incredibly energizing to see the effects of the helper's accurate empathy on themselves and on others.

We'd like to make an argument in favor of a more empathetic world. We believe that if we understood the value of showing others empathy as our first response, the world would be much more loving for all humans. By understanding what empathetic understanding really is, what it isn't, and how it is beneficial to you and to those around you, the world will be gentler and kinder. And if everyone was more empathetic, humanity would see much more loving connection.

What is Accurate Empathy?

Empathy differs from sympathy in that sympathy is a feeling of similarity with a person, whereas empathy is putting yourself in that person's spirit and trying to understand their perspective. Empathetic understanding is the idea of a gentle guess, "Putting yourself in someone else's being" and it comes with many benefits. **Listen deeply** for the whisper below the content. You need to be willing to be vulnerable. As we pursue the deepest silence and secrecy of another person while focusing upon what matters to them, we find a moment of peace and calmness in the moment where the body creates chemicals similar to the feeling of love. It is an anti-anxiety, naturally produced medication. This is the power of accurate empathy.

What Empathy Is Not

We often get confused; empathy is not weakness. It is a neutral act of seeking to truly understand another. Practice the principle: **We need to understand another fully before our need to be understood**. When paired with self-respect and compassionate boundaries, it becomes the most powerful tool of loving speech. Just because you can empathize with someone does not give them the right to keep hurting you. It is showing them that you understand their world – their thoughts and feelings – and with compassionate boundaries, it is an ability to help them to be in the process to *love fully*.

Benefits, Relationship Building

All too often we are in conflict, which often results in many of us only thinking only of our own needs. Our first thought is often a **righting reflex**. By being empathetic, in someone else's being, we show others that we care deeply and want to see the world from their perspective, thoughts, and feelings. Empathetic understanding builds emotional trust, understanding, and strengthens our connection in relationships. When you experience someone trying to see your perspective, you are sure to gain respect and genuine warmth for them. We can be assured this inspires others and ourselves to want to love well.

Self-Regulation

When we look at the world from someone else's point of view, when we see them from the heart, we are also looking at our thoughts and feelings and how they impact the people we are with in this moment. You would be surprised by how many people can't do empathetic understanding! Thinking about how our actions and words impact others is a form of empathy, and it is also self-regulation. It stops us from reacting into a right position. **To hold tightly a right position is to destroy the relationship**. This is a skill that is difficult to master and will create a much healthier you; physically, mentally, emotionally, spiritually, and sexually.

Mutuality

If we want people's respect, practice authentic empathetic understanding seeking accurate moments of deep connection. If we want to reduce the shame in our partners, friends, and family, practice empathy. It's the only antidote to trauma and oppression. If we want to change the community conditions that promote suffering, practice empathetic understanding. You will be surprised at how people will go out of their way to help and be present with you. Be sure to seek to understand the other first before your need to be understood. Empathy is not rage, nor does the action of empathetic understanding need to be done with the expectation of anything in return. It only gives back, creating self-empathetic talk and compassion within yourself.

The phrase, ***People are more willing to change when they are completely free not to change.*** is among those that are both true and nearly impossible to put into practice. How difficult is it as a helper to sit and watch someone injure themselves and still trust that this is their journey? Try this as a thought experiment when you are finding it hard not to have your hand on the steering wheel (unsolicited advice) as a helper. Imagine that you are on the passenger side of a vehicle and the person you are serving is driving the car and not very well. So, you get afraid, grab the handle, hit the imaginary brake, and bark at them. Everything you do in reaction (a righting reflex) to their poor driving makes them an even worse driver. Your goal is to let go of all would-be driving agency and your fears now and patiently wait for them to say, "Would you help me navigate?" There's no greater honor than such a question, to which your answer is not, "Yes, here's what you should do first." but rather, "What kind of support would you like right now?"

And remember to guard against letting open-ended questions devolve into endless curiosity, which can hurt the conversation. Another thought experiment: your relationship with a person is an emotional trust fund to which you make deposits with empathetic understanding. Every time you ask a question out of curiosity, you are taking a withdrawal from that fund, a problem since most people come to you already bankrupt around relationships. They are alone, possessing scarce emotional resources, and in need of *social capital*, which is the key to amplifying their confidence in their hopes and dreams and silencing their trauma whispers. Can you put enough deposits into their emotional trust fund so that they are no longer bankrupt? Remember the alternatives that your "pesky ego" suggests such as unsolicited suggestions, energetic reaction, advice about further education and resources likely won't ever be accepted as deposits by them.

To end on a hopeful note, though the trauma whisper seems ever-present, each of us also has a hopes and dreams whisper, which will get louder as you train. Practice your ear to hear it. In this more salutary whisper are at least three notes which, when amplified, combine into a melody – people want power and control over the destiny of their lives, they want to love and be loved, and they want to feel capable, have a purpose and a sense of belonging, have social capital. May we all be part of bringing this melody into the world.

Postscript: *I wish for each of you to get caught by the spirit of the love and peace in your heart... I have sadly injured some of my helping relationships by omission, anger, "pesky ego", and my isolation... I am truly sorry. I hope for your forgiveness...Thank you for being my teachers its you that echoes in this book.... I will continue to carry you in my heart each breathe even if my mind talks or has talked to me in other ways than love, empathy, and compassion...*

Listen deeply to the whisper,

Stephen 🖤

ABOUT THE AUTHOR

Stephen R. Andrew LCSW, LADC, CCS is a storyteller, consultant, community organizer and trainer who maintains a compassion-focused private practice and facilitates weekly men's, coed, women's, and Motivational Interviewing learning groups. He provides coaching and training domestically and internationally for social service agencies, health care providers, substance abuse counselors, criminal justice, and other groups on motivational interviewing, supervision, ethics for caring services professionals, men's work, and the power of group work. Stephen lives in Portland, Maine with his sweet wife Hilary, and is the proud father of Sebastian.

Making it happen is our commitment to the world ~50% of our profits will go to the (not- for- profit), AGAPE Inc., dedicated to providing support services and education to create compassionate solutions that strengthen our communities.

www.dignitymaine.com

Printed in the USA
CPSIA information can be obtained
at www.ICGtesting.com
CBHW030126110524
8110CB00010B/29

9 781088 113165